Edmund Hillary
& Tenzing Norgay

Terry Barber

FAMOUS
FIRSTS
SERIES

Edmund Hillary & Tenzing Norgay is published by
Grass Roots Press, a division of Literacy Services of Canada Ltd.

PHONE 1–888–303–3213
WEBSITE www.literacyservices.com

ACKNOWLEDGEMENTS

We acknowledge the financial support of the Government of Canada through the Book Publishing Industry Development Program (BPIDP) for our publishing activities.

We acknowledge the support of
the Alberta Foundation for the Arts
for our publishing programs.

Editor: Dr. Pat Campbell
Image research: Dr. Pat Campbell
Book design: Lara Minja, Lime Design Inc.
Book layout: Andrée-Ann Thivierge, jellyfish design

Library and Archives Canada Cataloguing in Publication

Barber, Terry, date
        Edmund Hillary & Tenzing Norgay / Terry Barber.

(Famous Firsts series)
ISBN 978-1-894593-65-6

        1. Hillary, Edmund, Sir. 2. Tenzing Norkey, 1914-1986. 3. Mountaineers--New Zealand--Biography. 4. Mountaineers--Nepal--Biography. 5. Readers for new literates. I. Title.

PE1126.N43B3643 2007   428.6'2   C2007-902785-7

Printed in Canada.

Contents

Mount Everest is 29,028 feet
(8,848 metres) above sea level.

Top of the World

Mount Everest is the world's highest mountain. For years, men try to reach the top. Many men die trying to reach the top. Many people think no one will ever reach the top.

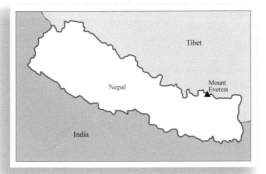

Mount Everest lies between Nepal and Tibet.

Edmund Hillary and Tenzing Norgay.

Top of the World

In 1953, two men reach the top of Everest. They become heroes to the world. One lives in Nepal. His name is Tenzing Norgay. The other man is from New Zealand. His name is Edmund Hillary.

Who do you think is the first man to reach the top?

A yak.

Tenzing Norgay

Tenzing Norgay is born in 1914. He grows up in a village. The village is 12,500 feet (3,810 metres) above sea level. Tenzing looks after **yaks**. This is a hard job for a child. It is hard to work at a high **altitude**.

Tenzing can speak seven languages. He never learns to read and write.

Tenzing Norgay, 1953.

Tenzing Norgay

Tenzing has a dream. He wants to reach the top of Everest. He works with climbers who share the same dream. Tenzing goes on six trips with climbers. They do not make it to the top of Everest.

Tenzing's mother calls Everest "The Mountain So High No Bird Can Fly Over It."

These Sherpa men carry heavy loads.

Tenzing Norgay

Tenzing is a Sherpa. Many Sherpa men help people climb in the **Himalayas.** The Sherpa people can work at high altitudes. Most Sherpa men are small and strong. They can carry heavy loads.

Most Sherpa families live in the mountain villages of Nepal.

A father and child walk in the hills of New Zealand.

Edmund Hillary

Ed Hillary is born in 1919. As a child, Ed loves to walk in the hills. He loves to read. He reads about people who love adventure. Ed is a quick learner. He skips two grades in school.

The hard path is often the best path.

Edmund Hillary

Ed's teen years are less happy. He feels restless. He does not do well in school. But Ed does find a sport he loves. He finds mountain climbing. Ed compares climbing to life. He thinks the easy path is not always the best path.

Ed Hillary looks up into the mountains.

Edmund Hillary

Ed knows mountain climbing is
dangerous. Still, he likes to climb. He
is in the fresh air. He sees great views.
He feels free. Mountain climbing
makes Ed feel more alive.

Edmund Hillary and Tenzing Norgay, 1953.

The Everest Team

Tenzing Norgay and Edmund Hillary. The two men share a **passion**. They love to climb mountains. They belong to the team that will reach the top of Everest. You could not pick two better people to work together.

Many people in Nepal and Tibet believe Everest is **sacred.**

The Everest team, 1953.

The Everest Team

In 1953, the British put together a team to climb Everest. John Hunt is the team's leader. There are 38 men on the team. The men depend on one another. Each person must have skills that help the team.

One climber says, "A team must move as one man to stand a chance of success."

23

Edmund Hillary puts on his special boots, 1953.

The Everest Team

The Everest team plans every detail of the trip. They take food that will not spoil. Tents must be sturdy so that the team sleeps well. Special boots are made to protect the climbers from the cold.

These Sherpa men wear oxygen masks.

Mount Everest, 1953

The team starts the trip in March
1953. They suffer at the high altitude.
The thin air makes it hard to breathe.
The thin air makes them feel lazy.
They don't want to eat. But they must
eat to stay strong.

Edmund Hillary uses a ladder to cross a crevasse.

Mount Everest, 1953

The trip is very dangerous. Snow and ice cover the mountain. The ice never melts. It takes the team five days to climb an ice fall. They use ladders to cross **crevasses** in the ice fall.

Many people who climb Everest get frostbite from the cold.

Hillary and Tenzing climb together.

Mount Everest, 1953

It is April 26. Hillary tries to jump over a crevasse. He falls in the crevasse. Tenzing saves his life. Hillary says, "Without Tenzing, I would have been finished today." The two men start to climb together every day. They trust each other.

Tenzing and Hillary rest on a ledge, May 28, 1953.

Mount Everest, 1953

The team leader chooses two men to climb to the top. He chooses Tenzing and Hillary. On May 28, the two men climb to 27,900 feet (8,504 metres). They rest on a ledge and shiver. It is -32° C. The wind roars.

Hillary and Tenzing must use oxygen when they climb and sleep.

Tenzing Norgay on the top
of Mount Everest, May 29, 1953.

Mount Everest, 1953

The next day, Hillary and Tenzing get up at 6:30 a.m. They climb 1,128 feet (344 metres) to reach the top. Tenzing says: "We stepped up. We were there. The dream had come true."

By 2007, 3,050 men and women reach the top of Everest. Over 200 people have died on the mountain.

Hillary and Tenzing make headlines.

After Everest

Tenzing and Hillary are the first men to climb Everest. They are heroes. They make headlines around the world. They get paid to speak and tell their story. They use their fame and money to make life better for the Sherpa people.

Sherpa woman from a mountain village.

After Everest

Hillary is grateful to the Sherpa guides. He knows the Sherpa guides made the climb a success. Hillary wants to help the Sherpa people. Hillary knows their lives are hard. Hillary knows their basic needs are not met.

Khymjung School—founded in 1961.

After Everest

Hillary asks, "Is there anything I can do?" The Sherpa people say, "We would like our children to go to school." Hillary and his friends work with the Sherpa people. In 1961, they build a school. Sherpa people are trained to teach in the school.

Hillary starts the Himalayan Trust. The trust has built 27 schools.

A statue of Tenzing Norgay outside the school.

After Everest

Tenzing uses his fame to help Sherpa people. He teaches at a school in India. He trains other Sherpas to be guides. The Prime Minister of India is happy. He tells Tenzing, "Now you will make a 1000 Tenzings."

Tenzing Norgay dies in 1986.

Edmund Hillary and Tenzing Norgay.

A Team Effort

Who was the first to set foot on the top of Everest? Tenzing or Hillary? Both say it does not matter. It was a team effort. Only one thing matters. Both men use their fame to help others.

Hillary says, "We shared the work, the risks, and the successes."

Glossary

altitude: the height about sea level.

crevasse: a deep open crack in the ice.

Himalayas: a large mountain range in south Asia.

passion: a strong feeling.

sacred: holy.

yak: an Asian ox.